Dedicated to my three amazing children who have taught me everything I know, and to my amazing grandchildren and future grandchildren.

I love you! I bless you! I thank God for you!

Published in Kansas City, Missouri, by keys4.3Dthinkers™

ISBN: 9781983978647

THE 7 KEYS TO

READING

READINESS

Unlocking the Doors to Learning

By: Karen Marie Kosloske
Schoeben M.Ed.SPEC
All Things Are Possible Education

PARENTS: Are you looking for the keys to unlock the doors to your PreK through 1st grade child's life-long learning? Are you looking for the keys to correcting your child's reversed, tilted letters or numbers that don't stay on the lines? Has your child met every developmental milestone? Is your child advanced in some areas and behind in others? This interactive story gives the 7 Keys needed to lay the foundation for learning and prevent academic failure. As your child masters each skill level and earns a key, they are forging the neuropathways needed to be a strong life-long learner. This is the first line of defense for all children, whether advanced, struggling with writing and reading issues, or those in between.

WHY 7 KEYS TO READING READINESS?

It is very important to lay the correct foundation for lifelong learning and success. It's critical for the brain to practice large motor skills and to follow directions in order to set the stage necessary for fine motor skills. Fine motor skills are used to sit at a desk, pay attention, understand, and have the short and long-term memory needed for reading, writing, and math readiness. This book helps lay the foundation.

I have created 7 Keys which will teach your child to see, hear, remember, and write correctly. These keys will prevent your child from writing with reversed, tilted, or "flying" letters or numbers, which occur when children don't use the lines as a guide to write, and thus they appear to be "flying in space".

Developmentally, preschool through first grade is when your child's brain is making the pathways for directionality, time, and space. So, if letters are flying or backwards, now is the time to change that through **Practice! Practice! Practice**! and giving **BIG REWARDS** as they master the skills of writing. Typically, if a child's letters and numbers are still backwards, tilted or flying by third grade, he/she usually will qualify for help with learning disabilities. **BUT NO MATTER WHEN YOU START WITH THESE KEYS, IT WILL STILL PRODUCE FRUIT.**

I ran into the mom of one my students in the grocery store a year after his therapy. She had a problem. She said, "I know I paid you to teach him to read, but now he's staying up late with a flashlight to read under the covers. I can't get him to stop!" And since then, he successfully made it through a competitive high school, achieved excellent grades so he could play sports, and earned a full scholarship into a top-ten school!

I have thousands of stories like this about children just like your child that I have collected over the last 40 years! Will you join my story? I love you. I bless you. I thank God for you. Remember ALL THINGS ARE POSSIBLE with Mama Kare is in your corner praying for you and your children. Share your story at www.atap-edu.com.

Who I am:

I am a mother, with 3 brilliant grown children, and 3 grandbabies to date. I have a master's degree in Special Education, and I've taught in orphanages, public schools, private schools and private practice since 1978. I have instructed several thousand children, those who were traditional learners and those on whom the schools and parents had given up hope. My children have had challenges: medical, emotional and academic. **They have overcome**, and they are the powerful ones. I have never met a child I couldn't teach to read! I have a story to tell.

Thank you for being a part of my story. I am eternally grateful for those of you who have spent countless hours editing and encouraging: Perfect Word Editing Services www.perfectwordediting.com, Viola Jackson, Daisy Burgan, Lauren Fraser, Mary, Nick and Erika Schoeben, Susan McClung, Jenn Townsley and The 7 Keys To Reading Readiness Mom's Focus Group (Krystal Evensen, Jessica Lima, Jackie Lugo, Anna Baker). Thank you all who have read through the edits and given your endorsement! Special thanks to Constance Ann Winter Kosloske, friend and long-time benefactor, and Mike and Lori Kosloske for letting your kids be the first to play the games and be in the prototype books!

Parents, teachers and therapists: I am so proud of you for taking the time to make a difference in the life of your child. You will not regret it and your future scholars will SOAR into their destiny, gifts and callings! Enjoy using this manual to kickstart your child's successful education. I love you! I bless you! I thank God for you!

Do you have any questions? Need specific tips? Contact me through www.atap-edu.com.

Karen Marie Kosloske Schoeben M.Ed.SPEC

Educational Therapist, Program Director:

All Things Are Possible Education

SOAR and Camp Genius

"Mama Kare"

Table of Contents:

Introduction

Before each key is a parent page in blue. Most of the blue words throughout the book are notes to parents and teachers and are not intended to be read aloud to the children.

After each key is a page in blue with ideas to "camp out" on, if needed, until your child acquires the skills needed to master that key.

Treat this Table of Contents like a checklist of skills that need to be conquered. Write the date of victory after each key in the margins and/or in the Table of Contents after each skill set mastered.

Are you ready to earn the keys to reading readiness?

Mama Kare has never met a child she couldn't teach to read! Stick with Mama Kare...she'll get you there! She's got the keys! Thousands of kids have earned their keys if you please! Now those kids can read and have everything they need! First things first...we need to get our brains ready! Get ready to...

1

Come on an adventure with me!

Once upon a time, in a land found in my imagination, there lived a King.

A Lion King.

He was not just any King. He was the King of *ALL* **the** kings! The Lord of *all* the lords.

The **MOST** POWERFUL!

The **MOST** HIGH in all the lands.

The **MOST** LOVING.

The **MOST** KIND.

The **MOST** FUN.

The **MOST** PLAYFUL.

The **MOST** COLORFUL in all the universe!

He and **HE ALONE** holds the keys to every book. HE wrote a book about you! And *even* a book about me! A book about how important we are to His kingdom! The book is our story, that tells us how we walk in our destiny, gifts and calling!

#1

The Ultimate Key: **Identity Key**

It unlocks the book of me!

Imagine a World

This little girl is using her

IMAGINATION.

She is being wrapped in love.

Can you use YOUR imagination...

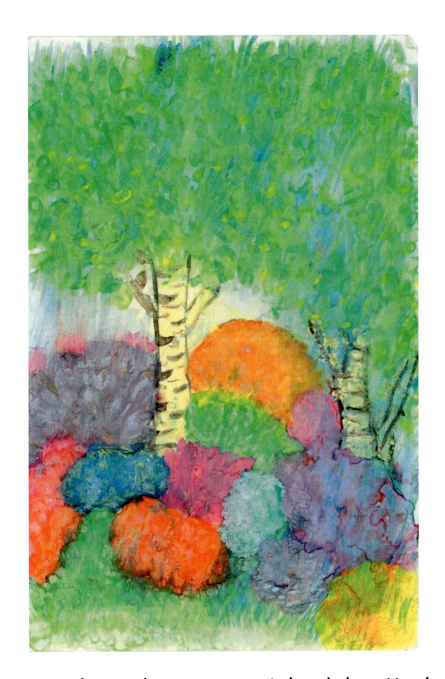

...to imagine a world with all the
brightest colors?

...and **ALL** the best songs?

Have you ever picked up a shell and put it to your ear?

Can you hear the ocean's song?

Imagine a world where you are not tired...

not hungry...

not hurt...

not sad...

not worried...

not scared...

It's all in a Book!

Child: I can't read.

Everything is *so* dark.

The book is locked!

It's so sad, the sky is crying!

The King:

I can help! Will you be brave? Will you put your trust in Me?

If you just call My name, I'll be there! Did you know that I have plans for you—plans for a future full of *hope?*

Close your eyes and let My words for your book sink deep in your heart.

Before the world was created, I thought about you. I placed visions and dreams in your heart! I formed you in your mama's tummy to be My friend... And guess what?

I whisper My mysteries to My friends!

OPEN YOUR EARS...

...to the mysteries of love, joy, forgiveness, peace and truth.

...to the mysteries of new games, new songs, new books, new jokes, and witty inventions to touch the hearts and lives of your friends, family and many more!

OPEN YOUR EYES...

You have gifts and talents that only YOU possess, and if you don't use these gifts and talents...

These new things won't be made!

NOW CLOSE YOUR EYES ONCE AGAIN...

Can you see with your imagination what you are going to do? What you will create?

No one can take your place.

THERE IS NO ONE

ELSE LIKE YOU!!!

You are a GIFT.

You are SPECIAL.

You are my precious TREASURE.

 Mama Kare: My friend Solomon said that the Lion will give *YOU* eyes to see and ears to hear. Do you want to hear?

Child: I want to hear the words of the book!

Mama Kare: My friend Isaiah also said that there will be a day when *YOU* will hear the words **of the Book and come out of darkness to** see. **Do you want to see?**

Child: **I want to come out of the darkness and see!**

I believe!

Please help me!

The Lion hears your cry and fills the dark places with....

LIGHT

Child: Hey! Everything was dark and now I can see! Who turned on the lights?

. . .

Child: **When will *I* be ready to read my story?**

First things first. Who are you?

The King:

I will tell you. You are a gift!

You are My *precious treasure*! You have eyes that see and ears that hear! You are My *masterpiece*, created for good works!

Mama Kare:

REPEAT AFTER ME TO EARN YOUR KEY!

(Parents: Please pause and let your child repeat after you say each line.)

I am a **GIFT**.

I am a precious **TREASURE**.

I have eyes that see and ears that hear!

I am God's **MASTERPIECE**, created for good works!

Mama Kare: **Your brain, just like every snowflake and every fingerprint, is different, SPECIAL, and a GIFT.**

17

Every brain learns differently. Your brain learns through your five senses, by what you...

SEE: Can you find your eyes?

HEAR: Can you find your ears?

TASTE: Can you find your tongue?

SMELL: Can you find your nose?

TOUCH: Can you find your hands? Where are your fingers?

Now find the **top** of your head.

That's where your brain is hiding!

Can you find your shoulders?

(Parents: Please have your children follow your lead as you point to each body part and show them direction words.)

Your head is **above** your shoulders.

Your knees are **below** your hips.

Your toes are hiding **in** your shoes, **below** your knees.

Your head is **on top**,

your hips are **in the middle**,

and your feet are **on the bottom**.

Did you show that you know who you are and can name your body parts?

Congratulations! You have earned your FIRST KEY! 🔑

Date of victory:_____

You are getting ready!

Are these things too hard?

Let's camp out here...

IF YOUR CHILD CANNOT NAME HIS/HER BODY PARTS, here are some ideas:

For body parts, play Simon Says, or sing 'Head, Shoulders, Knees and Toes'. Keep repeating the body part and pointing to, dancing, or singing about that body part. Silliness works! Shoulders are tough. You can say, "These are my shoulders. Can you say shoulders? Find your shoulders. Good. Great. Find your head. Fabulous. Find your shoulders. Find your head. Find your shoulders. Shoulders. Head. Shoulders. Head. You got it! See how smart you are!"

IF REPEATING 10 SYLLABLES IS TOO HARD, start with one syllable/sound and work your way up.

First things first: Has your child had a hearing screening? Can they hear all the sounds spoken?

Can they pronounce all the words, repeating back one word at a time?

Do they remember if you chunk two or three words together?

Do they remember if you chain the words?

I

I am

I am God's

I am God's mas

I am God's master

I am God's masterpiece

I am God's masterpiece create

I am God's masterpiece created

I am God's masterpiece created for

I am God's masterpiece created for good

I am God's masterpiece created for good works!

Dance! Sing! Be silly! Repeat. Repeat. Repeat. Do this day after day, until the path in the brain is firmly made! Still not happening? Watch the key video blog at www.atap.edu.com.

There are seven keys to earn before you are ready to read.

You have already earned the first key. Do you want to earn the keys to unlock the rest of the book?

There are six more to go!

When you have earned all seven keys, the book is unlocked, and you are ready to learn to read. Reading has two parts— **reading** the words and **hearing** the words of the book.

Dear Parents,

The most important skill in this is spatial orientation, which is knowing where the body is located in time and space. Directionality is key: knowing north, south, east, west or the equivalents up, down, left and right. The ATAP program uses the compass directions quite nicely, so if your child has a fairly good idea of left and right, work on that skill until it is solid, and then start to use the direction words together.

You can say: "North is the same as up. West is always left when you are facing north. East is always right when facing north. South is always down when looking at a map. Reading is always <u>top to bottom</u> (north to south) and <u>left to right</u> (west to east). Math is **always** top to bottom, <u>right to left</u> depending on what method you use. Is left (or west) always left when your eyes are closed? Is it always left when you are lying down? How about when you are facing the door? Or when you are facing the window? Concentrate on one direction at a time. Start with top or north and left or west. You can say, "We always start reading and writing at the top left-hand corner or the northwest edge of the page. This is not a surprise, it does not change, and it is always true."

Without this orientation to life and the page, children will never understand the written word, and will read wherever their eyes land. Some children naturally pick this up as you read to them and as they learn to decode. It's an unspoken rule. Our children need to be taught. The other concept that our children need to be taught is that object permanence does not apply to the letters of the alphabet. In other words, a child learns that no matter how you turn a ball, it is a ball. The ball can be half hidden under the bed, and it is still a ball. However, you cannot turn around letters, such as: d,b,p,q,g,n,h,u,m,w,f,j,t. If you do, they turn into other letters.

Most children discover this on their own terms or when introduced to an Orton based phonics program. Some see it when they are introduced to cursive writing. Many educators skip or touch lightly upon directionality skills and incorrectly assume children have mastered them. For example, I've had children that I thought had mastered their directions, only to find out that they did not know up, down, left and right with their eyes closed, while lying on the floor, in different rooms, or outside.

These are the same children who, after receiving extensive visual and educational therapy, still reverse their letters and words. These are the children for whom I have written this program. This program provides keys to prevent learning difficulties. Not all the children who have missed these foundational pieces have difficulty learning. <u>But, all the children who have difficulty learning have missed one of these foundational pieces. I have discovered in the Educational Therapy setting that if I go back and rebuild the pieces that were missing in the foundation of learning, children will quickly jump up to grade level.</u> I am now placing this powerful tool in your hands: a checklist, a set of keys to unlock those foundational skills needed to learn. If learning comes naturally and easily for your child, this checklist ensures a solid learning foundation. If learning does not come easy for your child, this checklist will help you build that solid foundation. Don't get overwhelmed! Work on one skill at a time. Have fun and keep records so you and your child can see the results.

#2

Direction Key

Are you ready to earn your

SECOND KEY? 🔑 🔑

Before you learn to read, your brain must be able to know the direction words and be able to follow four-part instructions.

To earn the next key, you must know and follow direction words and know the colors.

Follow these directions:

- Put your hands on **top** of your head. Put your hands under your **bottom**.

- Show me your **left** hand. Show me your **right** hand.

- Put your hands **in** your pockets or pretend pockets. Take your hands **out** of your pockets.

- Put your hands **above** the table. Put your hands **below** the table.

- Put your hands **down** by your sides. Put your hands **up** in the air.

- Put your hands **behind** your back. Put your hands **in front** of your tummy.

- Get **closer** to the person reading these directions.

- Get **farther** from the person reading these directions.

Now let's work our way up to four-part instructions.

- **Stand up.** (Sit back down.)

- **Stand up and turn around.** (Sit back down.)

- **Stand up, turn around and walk to the window.** (Sit back down.)

- **Stand up, turn around and walk to the window and say, "Good Morning!"**

Can you find and name all the colors?

Point to and name **blue**, **red**, **green**, **yellow**, **orange**, **pink**, **purple**, **black**, **brown**, **gray**, **and** white.

Did you show that you know direction words and colors, and can follow instructions?

Congratulations! You have earned your SECOND KEY! Find and circle 2 keys!

Date of victory: _____

You are getting ready!

Are these things too hard?

Let's camp out here...

Do really camp out here... For a week, let every game and every word that comes out of your mouth have to do with top, bottom, left and right. Have your kids make up an obstacle course with specific top, bottom, left and right directions. Get a pad of sticky notes and label mirrors, doors, and windows with top, bottom, left and right. Make up games and songs... while setting the table, brushing your teeth. For every direction you give!

Establish:

Writing hand: left or right hand?

Kicking foot: left or right foot?

Throwing hand: left or right hand?

Take a paper towel roll cardboard tube and have them spot something across the room, using it like a telescope: left or right eye?

To help them memorize, use bracelets or stickers, or write with permanent marker on their dominant hand: L for left and R for right.

Once they have it memorized, have them close their eyes and ask them to show you their right hand. Ask them to lay down. "Is that still your right hand? With your eyes closed and your eyes open, that's still your right hand? No matter which way you turn, no matter what time of day, no matter what day, that is still your right hand?" Process with them until they discover for themselves. Right hand. Right foot. Right eye. Right side. Right is always right. Left is always left.

You can still move on to the other keys, but do not stop focusing on left and right until that path is firmly established in the brain!

Have fun and take your time with the direction key! We all know adults that don't know their directions...that's why I started early with my own kids. Even if it takes years. ALL THINGS ARE POSSIBLE education with Mama Kare knows that this is possible. If you don't quit...you win!

Still not happening? Watch video blog to see a demonstration at www.atap.edu.com.

#3

Large Motor Key

Dear Parents,

I have found when I start teaching jumping rope at this developmental age, that by the time children can jump rope they will be reading fluently. Jumping rope, riding a bike, and swinging are skills that require a lot of communication between many parts of the brain. So does being able to have their eyes follow a skilled reading pattern, decode, remember each letter sound, blend sounds, remember word patterns, understand vocabulary, pronounce sounds, read, focus, comprehend, connect with what they are reading, and store sight words in their memory. This takes a lot of communication in the brain! I can teach every skill needed to read, but at some point the brain needs to blend all those skills together, and take off the training wheels to begin reading on its own. It is much like a child riding a two-wheeler for the first time without a parent holding on and helping with balance.

Watch the video "The Learning Brain" by yourself, with your children and even with your spouse. Stop, start and discuss and interpret at your childrens' understanding level.

www.atap-edu.com

Focus on the bike analogy in the video. You will need this analogy to explain to your family the importance of the next key and its importance in the foundation for life-long learning. This key may take days, months and even years to master. Practice, practice, practice. Break every task down to its smallest part and start there.

#3

Large Motor Key

Are you ready to earn the

Third KEY? 🔑 🔑 🔑

Can you do these things?

- Crawl

- Walk

- Jump with both feet (count to ten)

- Walk a line or balance beam

- Stand on left foot (count to ten)

- Stand on right foot (count to ten)

- Hop on left foot (ten times and count to five)

- Hop on right foot (ten times and count to five)

- Skip (skip across the room)

- Jump rope (ten times or go through the motion of jumping rope, practicing until all 4 quadrants of the brain coordinate and they can jump rope for real)

Did you show that you can use large motor skills? Did you follow directions?

Find and circle 3 keys!

Date of victory: _____

Congratulations! You have earned your
THIRD KEY! 🔑 🔑 🔑

Are these things too hard?

Let's camp out here...

Now <u>really</u> watch the video "The Learning Brain" by yourself, with your children and even with your spouse. Stop, start and discuss and interpret at your childrens' understanding level. <u>www.atap-edu.com</u>

Focus on the bike analogy in the video. You will need this analogy to explain to your family the importance of the next key and its importance in the foundation for life-long learning. This key may take days, months and even years to master. Practice, practice, practice. Break every task down to its smallest part and start there.

For example: With jumping rope, start with holding the rope correctly. Then progress to going through the motion of jumping rope, placing the rope behind the feet and twirling the rope over the head and stepping over the rope. Congratulate them. Then graduate to hopping over the rope, then swinging the rope overhead and timing it to jump over the rope in one motion.

Still not happening? Go to www.atap-edu.com for key video blog.

#4

Eye Captain Key

Dear Parents,

Before your child is ready to read, you need to determine that they can remember things.

- Can they match four symbols, four numbers, and four letters? This is visual memory, visual discrimination, and visual matching.

- Can they remember and say four numbers and four letters? This is auditory memory, auditory discrimination, and auditory matching.

- Can they draw basic lines and shapes? This is visual motor coordination, and visual motor memory.

Before a child can discriminate numbers and letters, they need to be able to smoothly track with their eyes without losing the target. Take an object and have your child hold his/her head still while following the vertical, horizontal, diagonal and circular movement of the object, as you move it from place to place in the air with your hand. This is visual tracking.

#4

The Eye Captain Key

Are you ready to earn the **Fourth KEY**?

🔑 🔑 🔑 🔑

Now that your brain can follow directions and master large motor skills, your eyes need to do exercises to get in shape for reading. You also need to build your memory muscles.

Before you are ready to read, you need to show that your eyes can remember things.

- Can you match four symbols, four numbers, and four letters?

- Can you remember and say four numbers and four letters?

- Can you draw basic lines and shapes?

Can you point to the symbol or letter that is different in each line?

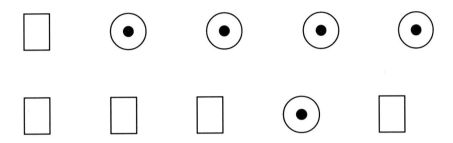

I L I I I I I I

O O O O D O O O

C C C G C C C C

H H H N H H H H

1 I I I I I I I I

C C C C C S C C C

On each line, can you find a match for the letter or letters in the first box?

a	o	a	u	e
ab	ba	ah	ab	ob
dad	add	dab	bad	dad
spot	tops	step	spot	top
from	form	torm	morf	from
girl	gril	girl	irgl	gilr
sale	cale	zale	sale	sole

Handedness:

Parents: Ask the child to draw the shape. Watch which hand they draw with and which box they choose to draw in.

Have your child look at each number one at a time for 5 seconds to memorize. Then cover the number and have them write each number.

94   38   527

_____
- -
_____

169   4987   3641

_____
- -
_____

Have your child look at each letter group one at a time for 5 seconds to memorize. Then cover the letters and have them write those letters. (Goal: work up to 4 letters and numbers, and by Jr High, 9 letters and numbers.)

pt   sz   wmo

_____
- -
_____

odc   qzts   vypl

_____
- -
_____

Did you show that your eyes and memory muscles are strong and ready to start reading?

Find and circle 4 keys!

Date of victory: _____

Congratulations! You have earned your

FOURTH KEY! 🔑🔑🔑🔑

Are these things too hard?

Let's camp out here...

To help your child earn the Eye Captain Key:

Play pirates, and using a cardboard or paper tube, have your children play 'I Spy' by spotting things across the room. Use your color and direction words: top, bottom, left, right, in, out above, below, down, up, behind, in front. Here is a variation to the 'hotter/colder game': use the words "closer" and "farther". This is called <u>figure ground discrimination</u> and is used in hidden picture puzzles found in the Highlight magazines, I Spy books, and Where's Waldo books.

Play "Statues" and have one child run an obstacle course while the others follow, only using their eyes to follow, not moving their heads. Make it even sillier and see if the obstacle runner can make the statues laugh. This is called <u>visual tracking</u>. Watch for smooth eye movements.

First Things First

If your child cannot discriminate and track, you need a developmental eye exam. Still not happening? Go to www.atap-edu.com for a key video blog.

#5

Tell Me All About It Key

Dear Parents,

Please ask your child the questions on the following page. To practice, have them trace over your numbers and letters as they answer each question. You can also have them trace in different colors. I call that "Rainbow Writing".

Your child should have these verbally memorized by 1st grade. Writing these from memory will come by second grade but start practicing now.

#5

Tell Me All About It Key

Are you ready to earn your **FIFTH KEY**?

Parent: Please ask your child the following questions. To practice, have your child trace over your numbers and letters as they answer your question. They should have these verbally memorized by 1st grade. Writing these from memory will come by second grade but start practicing now.

Can you say your first, middle, and last name?

_____

_____

_____

Can you remember your address? (Use a familiar song and replace the words with the address to help your child memorize his/her address.)

_____

_____

_____

_____

_____

_____

Can you remember your phone number?

_____

_____

_____

Can you repeat numbers, letters, and words?

Repeat after me to earn your key!

Parents: Read the numbers and letters to your child without letting your child peek, so they are remembering instead of reading the numbers and letters with you.

94	38	527	169
4987	3641	pt	sz
wmo	odc	qzts	vypl

Parents: Child listens only to parent and repeats each phrase. The goal is to work up to four words.

dog – boy

man – cat

ear – coat – key

boat – glass - egg

snow – king – back – lake

light – horse – doll – swing

Did you show that you can repeat words?

Find and circle 5 keys!

Date of victory_____

Congratulations! You have earned your

FIFTH KEY! 🔑 🔑 🔑 🔑 🔑

You are so close! Keep going!

Are these things too hard?

Let's camp out here...

PRACTICE repeating back letters

PRACTICE repeating words

PRACTICE repeating sentences

Still not happening?

Go to www.atap-edu.com for key video blog and link to start HEARBUILDER, EAROBICS AND/OR BRAINBUILDER.

Keep practicing! If you don't quit...you win!

#6

Clock Time Key

Parents: Please use any model of an analog clock you have on hand or draw one on a piece of paper.

Before your child is ready to read, you need to show that they can remember things such as numbers.

To see what they know, they are going to play a game called Clock Time. In this game you can use a clock to:

- count to 12 or even 60
- match numbers
- name numbers
- show objects of numbers 0 to 12 (one-to-one correspondence)

Goal: The goal of this activity is for the child to be able to **demonstrate** the ability to count, recognize numbers, and understand one-to-one correspondence.

#6

Clock Time Key

Are you ready to earn the **SIXTH KEY**?

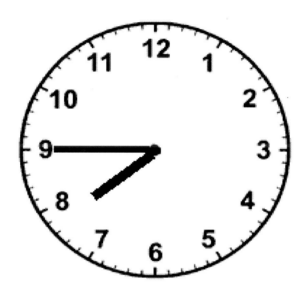

Using a clock helps let you know where you are in time and space. To earn this key, you need to be able to:

- count to 12 or even 60

- match numbers

- name numbers 1-12

1. Can you count as high as you can for me?

2. On each line, can you find a match for the number or numbers in the first box?

7	1	4	7	1
96	99	96	66	69
253	555	553	235	253
814	814	418	148	841
1012	1021	2012	1012	0112

3. Can you tell me the name of these numbers?

1   4   7   8   5   2

9   6   3   10   11   12

4. Can you show me how many fingers for each number?

9   6   3   10   1   4

7   8   5   2

5. Can you write 0 1 2 3 4 5 6 7 8 9 10 11 12?

_____

_____

_____

_____

Did you show that you can count, match, write and name numbers, and show number values?

Find and circle 6 keys!

Date of victory_____

Congratulations! You have earned your

SIXTH KEY! 🔑🔑🔑🔑🔑🔑

You are so close! Keep going!

Are these things too hard?

Let's camp out here...

Count everything! Use steps, Cheerios, grapes, blocks, until your child realizes that every number stands for that many objects. Get a big clock and count the numerals, then count the seconds, then count by fives.

PRACTICE

PRACTICE

PRACTICE

Still not happening?

Go to www.atap-edu.com for key video blog and link to start **HEARBUILDER, EAROBICS OR BRAINBUILDER.**

#7

ABC Key

Dear Parents,

All the skills taught with each key have been laying the foundation so that your child can see, hear, remember, and write correctly without reversed, tilted, or flying letters or numbers.

Developmentally, preschool through first grade is when your child's brain is making the pathways for directionality, time, and space. So, if letters are flying or backwards, **NOW** is the time to reach them through **Practice! Practice! Practice!** and **BIG REWARDS** when they have mastered their writing skills. If their letters and numbers are still backwards, tilted or flying by third grade, they usually qualify for help with reading and writing issues in a school setting.

So, take your time talking about what we call the Skyline Letters (See page 66). Letters should start at the top and go down to what I call the Sand Line. Some children will draw a number or letter differently every time. As an Educational Therapist, this is when I start strategies to prevent academic failure. Teach them to draw the letter or number the same way each time. Teach them that there is a top and a bottom, a left and a right. The letter "b" is the hardest. *FOCUS ON THE 'B', AND ONCE THE DIRECTION OF THE 'B' IS CORRECT, THE 'D', 'P', 'Q', AND 'G' FALL INTO PLACE.* Interestingly, many other countries teach cursive first and have a lower incidence of dyslexia.

Here's what you can say: "This the letter 'b'. Trace the letter 'b'. See how it drops from the sky, bounces off the sand, bounces back up, and says its sound 'buh-buh-buh-buh' (/b/), as in 'bounce'?" Teach that there is only one way to write the 'd'. Here's what you can say: "This the letter 'd'. Trace the letter 'd'. See how it starts like a 'c', stays in the ocean until the end, then goes up to the sky, and says its sound 'duh-duh-duh-duh' (/d/), as in 'dog'?" Spend time now so that your future scholars can SOAR into their destiny, gifts and calling!

This next section is going to take lots of 'extra love' for their emotional gas tanks: Hugs! Treats! Rewards!

Take the Love Languages quiz at the link below so that you can fill... fill... fill... up their emotional gas tank to overflowing! www.atap-edu.com

#7

ABC Key

Are you ready to earn the **SEVENTH KEY?**

You need to show that you can:

1. Write and name the letters of the alphabet.
2. Match the letters and their names.
3. Match the letters and their names and say their first sounds.

There are only **26 letters** in the alphabet, yet they can look so different, from upper case to lower case, print to cursive and oh so many fonts! (Like a = a)

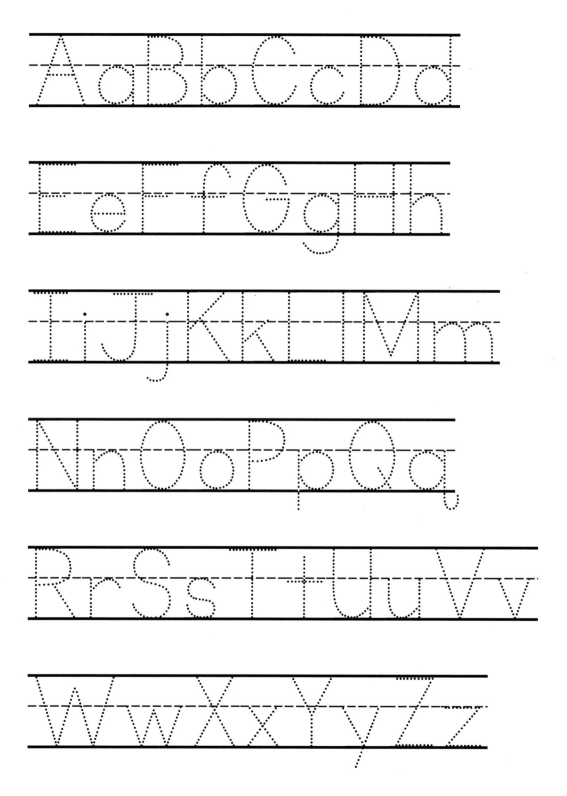

Aa Bb Cc Dd Ee

Ff Gg Hh Ii Jj Kk

Ll Mm Nn Oo Pp

Qq Rr Ss Tt Uu

Vv Ww Xx Yy Zz

There are so many games and puzzles and School Zone workbooks that you can pick up from every grocery store and bookstore. What they don't teach is that there are over 100 letter and sound combinations! We are just going to focus on single letters and first sounds. Teach the short sounds for the vowels and the first sounds for consonants: a=apple, e=egg, i=igloo, o=octopus, u=umbrella, y=yellow. c=cat, f=fish, g=goat, s=silly

Aa Bb Cc Dd Ee

Ff Gg Hh Ii Jj Kk

Ll Mm Nn Oo Pp

Qq Rr Ss Tt Uu

Vv Ww Xx Yy Zz

ABC Beach

- The lines for writing are just like the beach. The bottom line is where the water meets the sand or beach. Find and touch the **Sand Line.**

- The big or capital letters all touch the sand **and** touch the sky. Find and touch the **Sky Line.**

- The baby or lowercase letters have their own special rules. Most of them stay in the ocean. Find and touch the **Ocean Line.**

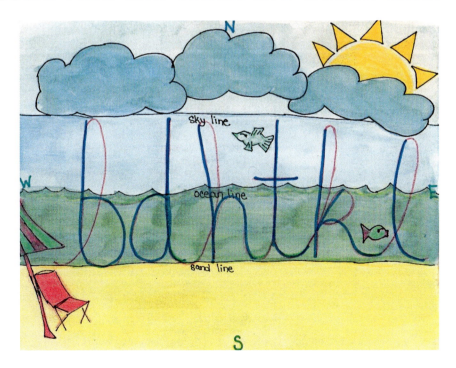

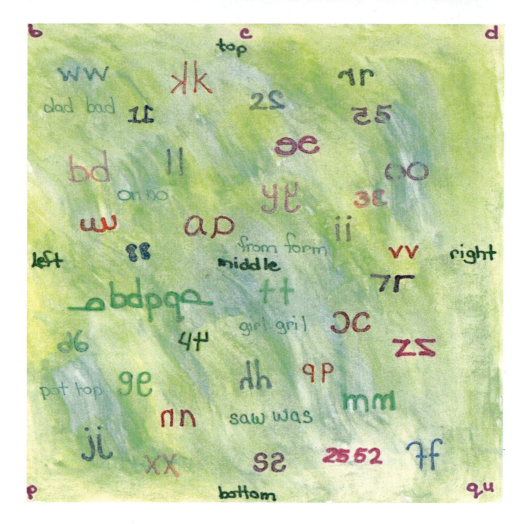

A key is a key no matter which way it turns, but a letter is not a letter no matter which way it turns. Letters have a top and a bottom, a left and a right, and they should be written the same way every time. Can you find the 'real' letter and number in the picture above?

Parents: You can say, "Can you find the real 'a'?" Then proceed through the alphabet. Then work through the numbers. For older students, I have included the most commonly misread words. Use this as a warm up for school activities daily. This does not need to be mastered to earn the key but should be mastered by 1st grade.

The Sky Guys

Only the tall letters can go all the way up and touch the sky. The letter 'f' is a Sky Guy in print and both Sand & Sky in cursive. Write the Sky Guys and say their names.

b   d   h   k   l   t

_____

_____

_____

The Ocean Guys

All the blue short letters live in the ocean.

They touch the sand and go up to the waves.

(From cursive to print: the e, r, s, & z are the only letters that get a little crazy.)

Write the Ocean Guys and say their names.

a c e m n o r s u v w x z

The Sand Guys

Certain "baby letters" get to go play in the sand. In print, 'f' is a Sky Guy, and in cursive, it's both a Sky Guy and a Sand Guy.

Write the Sand Guys and 'f'. Say their names

g j p y q

(q, who never ever goes anywhere without his friend u)

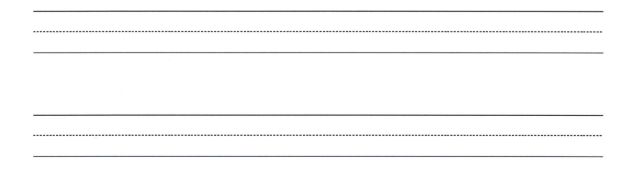

Say the names of the letters.

J N B V C Z

X U L K P M

H G F D S R

A P O I U G

Y T R E W Q

Say the name and first sounds of the letters.

Teach the short sounds for the vowels a=apple, e=egg, i=igloo, o=octopus, u=umbrella, y=yellow

a   s   d   f   g   u

h   j   k   l   p   e

o   l   u   y   t   r

r   e   w   q   m   t

n   b   v   c   x   z

Did you show that you can match, say sounds, write, and name the letters of the alphabet?

Find and circle 7 keys!

Date of victory: _____

Congratulations! You have earned your
SEVENTH KEY!

You are ready to learn to read!

You did it! I'm so proud of you! I knew you could do it! Thank you for working so hard! Now the Book is unlocked!

Did you see that there are six more keys hidden in the picture? Can you find them and circle them? These keys unlock the door for your next adventure ...the adventure of learning to read!

Congratulations! You are ready to learn to **read**, and **hear** the words of the Book," says the Lion.

I HAVE EARNED MY KEYS

I AM READY TO READ!

The sky is so happy! The first book is unlocked...

Your family is smiling!

Mama Kare is smiling!

She believes in you!

She's so proud of you!

Your brain is so smart!

Your future is so bright!

You are going to need your sunglasses!

You are **are** ready to learn to read. You **do** have the keys! It feels **so** good learning new things! You are **so** smart! So now, anyone can teach you.

If you want, I can teach you right now!

In my next adventure, I'm going to introduce you to all the friends who taught me how to read. Look for Mama Kare in the SOAR program at thedanielacademy.com, ALLTHINGS ARE POSSIBLE EDUCATION, CAMP GENIUS, and KEYS4.3DTHINKERS PRODUCT LINE for her next books and educational products.

Find me on Facebook, Karen Marie & ALL THINGS ARE POSSIBLE Education, Keys4.3Dthinkers or www.atap-edu.com to get connected. You can initiate the process of full testing for customized curriculum if needed, or to get your copy of Mama Kare's reading and writing fluency curriculum. Contact me at www.atap-edu.com

Prayer #1

Mama Kare's prayer for you is that the angels protect your destiny, your calling, and your future full of hope. She prays for your brain:

- that there is perfect health and wholeness, nothing missing, nothing lacking
- that the DNA and the RNA, the cells and all the synapses function in the order that God created them to function
- that the bad memory branches break off, fall to the ground and have no power over you
- that your memory branches get washed with the truth of who you are.

Mama Kare prays that you make good choices:

- that you pick the right friends
- that you use your gifts and talents
- that you have a strong voice, strong heart, strong mind and strong body
- that you will know when to follow and when to lead
- that you listen and obey God's voice and your parents' voice, and that you respect your teachers

Prayer #2

Children, embrace the truth! I delight in you. You are a gift. You are special. You are God's workmanship, His masterpiece! I promise to pray for you and help you:

- design your programs
- empower you—the leaders of tomorrow—to embrace your gifts and calling, to use your voice, to take a stand, to fill your minds and think about those things that are: true, honest, just, well-spoken of, pure, lovely, excellent, noble, reputable, authentic, compelling, gracious, the best, not the worst, the beautiful things to praise

May the joy of the Spirit of Truth be your strength! May your mind be so full of these things that there is room for nothing else. I love you! I believe in you! Walk in the hope of your calling! Call on and walk in the Truth. You are a leader and not a follower, above and not beneath! Your brain is uniquely wired for the dreams and visions God has placed in your heart. Take your place! Walk in your inheritance! Your future is so bright, you're going to need sunglasses!

Dear IEP Parents, parents of children diagnosed with developmental disabilities:

SLOW AND STEADY WINS THE RACE. Just concentrate on and give extra time for each developmental milestone and each key, even if they are at a slower pace initially. Your children are the leaders of the future. There is no ceiling to what they will do.

7 Keys to Reading Readiness is mandatory for children coming from homes with a history of reading or writing issues, or diagnoses such as dyslexia, dyspraxia, dysgraphia, ADD, ADHD, Asperger's, Autism or learning disabilities. Temple Grandin (educator, scientist, writer, biologist, and prominent advocate for the autistic community), has found that the genetic markers for autism and genius are the same, just to varying degrees. This proves to me that you can never start too young! What I've known all along is true! That every child has gifts and every child has challenges. When a preschool student is struggling, and you give them the right tools, you may just be training and equipping the next Albert Einstein. That is why regardless of whether my students come to me ahead of their peers or behind their peers, I always teach some form of the 7 Keys to Reading Readiness. These skills are just that foundational to the learning process.

My students labeled with dyslexia or just with dyslexia symptoms have gone on to be professional dancers, musicians, CEOs of Fortune 500 companies, teachers, authors, pastors, inventors, EMTs, firefighters, nurses, CNAs and athletes, because they are smart and they think outside the box. Once I explain to these creative 3D thinkers that letters only go one way, and when they can recognize the "b" instantaneously, they are free to be brilliant! Set up your child to be brilliant, too and give them the skills they need to Unlock the Doors to Learning and be successful in school!

If you are starting with young children, spend time and be diligent now so that you can avoid the dyslexia diagnosis, and your children can be free to read, create and invent.

IMPORTANT: There can be sensorimotor issues to overcome before your child has the attention span to sit down to learn paper/pencil activities. Early childhood programs are superior at working on all developmental milestones and many children then test out of services. But there are children who still need to work on these developmental milestones. Many school aged special education programs leave that work to the more qualified speech and language, physical, and occupational therapists. Unfortunately, if the student's IQ is measured too low, in many school districts the very students who need the services the most will not qualify or will have limited time with the very therapists that can literally help raise their IQ. This may be controversial to some, but I have seen, time and time again, that focusing on the 7 Keys to Reading Readiness creates the neuropathways needed for learning breakthrough, regardless of age. With God ALL THINGS ARE POSSIBLE. That is why I have written this book. You can do this! Parents, you have the power in the IEP process. If you find a professional that impacts your child, bless them, and learn from them. But I bless you to believe and remember that YOU are your child's best teacher and advocate!

AUTHOR'S NOTE

Over 20 years ago, I took the reading readiness section of the <u>Brigance Learning Inventory</u> and noticed that if a student didn't have all those skills by 3rd grade, they qualified for a learning disability. No exceptions. So, over time, I started screening, and then teaching reading readiness skills. I started with my own children, as I had three under 5 years old, and included every child I was tutoring who was struggling in school. Over the years I have developed many handmade games as screening tools. I went to publish these games and my editor said it that it read more like a testing manual or kit. She said to take it into the community and see what the moms thought. I did. The kids loved it! But the parents were intimidated.

So, I went back to the drawing board. I was working in the heart of Kansas City when I wrote this story for the kids. I saw their potential and wanted to prevent academic failure. The children gathered around my laptop as they earned a cheer and a "congratulations you have just earned a key" for each developmental skill mastered. No prizes. No treats. No rewards. Just the competition and reward of mastering a skill. Two days later the staff at the shelter called and told me that a little girl wanted to finish the next skill and earn the next key! I had not written the next key yet, but I knew I had a hit with the kids!

Next, one of my gifted business families had a little one that had watched her brothers and sisters work on skills with me for several years. She explained that she had waited her 'whole' life for me to work with her. She was next. I finished all seven keys and at four years old, she had mastered her skills and had 'earned' her keys. I think at this point I sketched little keys on an index card. On earning the 7th key she asked, "Is the sky happy now?" I had forgotten about the 'book being locked and it being so sad the sky was crying' in the beginning of the story. She didn't! She was hooked in the story, truly invested! I drew her a happy sky. By her 5th birthday she had written her first little story and read it to her grandparents on her actual birthday!

Then I thought, how do I convey what a huge developmental milestone this is to the mothers? So I wrote little introductions to each key. We called for mom and she pulled her daughter onto her lap as I read the story and described the skills that her daughter had now mastered! She cried! I had found the words to reach the hearts of the mothers!

Two years later, my friend pulled together a homeschool moms focus group. They helped me change the format. They suggested a '**2 minute why**' before each key and '**what to do if your child can't master a key**' after each key, links for more activities, key color sheets, a color book, and a video blog for the more difficult keys. The book is now formatted for the moms to easily use and is officially mother approved! I'm working on all the links and future activities, books and coloring books! Thank you: **Susan McClung, Krystal Evensen, Jessica Lima, Jackie Lugo, and Anna Baker**

The home stretch! As I mentioned before, everything I need to know about education I have learned from my children. They grew up in the ALL THINGS ARE POSSIBLE Learning Centers and Camps. They have seen my mistakes and they have experienced these Keys in action. I am overwhelmed by their belief in me and the importance of these Keys. I have been blessed and encouraged by their dedication to the excellence of this project and their attention to detail. They have used their gifts to help me clarify, summarize and highlight the important things that children's hearts need to hear. If I only had room for three endorsements, these three mean the most to me:

"This book is for everyone regardless of background, age, educational history, and without prejudice. Come with your challenges; and with the **right keys** for the **right doors** you can turn those challenging areas into strength and thriving!" **Erika Schoeben, mom, gifted 1-2 year old CEC Teacher**

"What she said." **Nick Schoeben, entrepreneur, gifted in sales**

"I'm so proud of my mom!" **Mary Schoeben, mom, gifted in customer service**

WHAT OTHERS ARE SAYING:

"I love this book. Karen is a genius when it comes to communicating with children. The illustrations are beautiful, and the messages are thought provoking and encouraging." **Marsha Huber, Ph.D., award winner in 'Teaching Excellence', 'Mentoring', and 'Innovation in Education'. Visiting Faculty scholar at Harvard University researching how the brain works in learning.**

"I wish I had this at the beginning of the last school year. Mary parents asked for resources to use to help get their children ready for Kindergarten screening. I would put this book in every parent's hand." **Judy Hauber, Preschool Teacher.**

The 7 Keys to Reading Readiness is **POWERFUL** because it gives parents and teachers common language. Children's chances of success are greatly enhanced when parents and teachers have common goals and expectations. So now they can be working on the same keys together. Karen has masterfully created a common tool kit for everyone who is invested in children reaching their potential! For the homeschool parent, it basically gives them their entire curriculum in one beautiful story. **Mim Sweigar, Retired Preschool Teacher, Elementary School Principal and Barb Shoup, Retired Preschool Teacher.**

"The 7 Keys to Reading Readiness is easy to read and practically helpful for yours and my child, whatever their skill level. Karen Schoeben's wide experience of many years and her love of children is evident throughout the fabric of her book. Along with Karen's heart for prayer and trust that God our Creator has uniquely and perfectly crafted the heart and mind of every child, the book is based upon years of care and practical investment into the lives of many children. The all-important theme of positive reinforcement and speaking encouragement and affirmation over our children is woven skillfully into the pages. Finally, though many books are written about many ideas, it is not often that an educator/practitioner backs up their innovation with an invitation to the reader to contact them for further help!" **Lelonnie Hibberd, Kindergarten Teacher, Elementary School Chaplain, The Daniel Academy.**

First of all, I don't say enough how blessed we are to have met you and get to work with you...just not enough words to express this. Thank you for being faithful to try again and reformat and rewrite "games" and THIS BOOK!

I LOVE this version/format of the book! It's easy to understand and follow! So much so that I cried. I feel that this book is the basics of working with Ms. Karen in a nutshell (especially with your prayers in the back!). It makes it clearer on how I can help Deborah (and Elijah) and the core of what you've been working on with Deborah all these years. Now I can finally see how all the curriculum, programs, and resources you've been using work together and what areas they strengthen) This book really really has your gift and love in it! I feel like I'll have more to say in the days to come. I'm just curious, did you use the comic sans font on purpose? It really bothered me until I went and briefly googled what font types are best for children and dyslexia :) (Mama Kare: Thank you your feedback. It validates the weeks I spent 20 years ago finding a font that had the right letter formation. The focus group didn't love the font and I think we a found a new favorite that I will use in this series and my reading and writing fluency curriculum. The only letter that is off is: a, a, a so we will just need to teach the differences.)

I am the mom Karen's IEP parent letter addresses at the back of this book. My 10-year-old daughter is one of those kids who would have fallen through the gaps without Mama Kare's genius and gifts. Years of chasing a diagnosis made it hard to define and measure all the "developmental delays" my daughter displayed, much less get her the help she truly needed. *We live in a time where more and more studies are showing the plasticity of our brains; how amazing the brain can be at changing itself! There is hope that these delays are no longer ceilings for our children.* However, it can be an expensive journey and incredibly overwhelming for a parent to know where to start. If that's you, START HERE! The affordable, easy-to-follow, and foundational tools introduced to parents in this book are like having brief meetings with a visual, auditory, speech, occupational, physical, and educational therapist all in one place. The neural pathways this book builds are key for ANY child. **Jenn Townsley, Mom of 6, Powerful Entrepreneur, amateur researcher of neuroplasticity and quantum physics.**

The 7 Keys to Reading Readiness is a gift to every parent of reading-age children. Karen Schoeben "Mama Kare" skillfully guides both parent and child through the many fundamental requirements for a child's brain to tackle reading successfully. This book is a gift, as it arms parents with knowledge and understanding of their child's needs, thus avoiding common pitfalls and struggles resulting from ignorance. Your children may be earning "Keys" to unlock a world of reading, but this book truly provides parents the keys to loving and helping their children through every learning curve. As a parent of a child nearing preschool age, I am so grateful to be aware of these 7 Keys from the very beginning. Thank you Mama Kare!

Katy Hunt, mom.

Here are some keys for your children to color, cut out, and display. Or you could put a ribbon through for them to wear as a necklace.

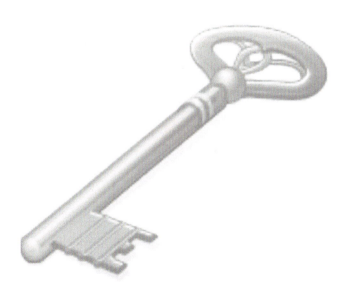

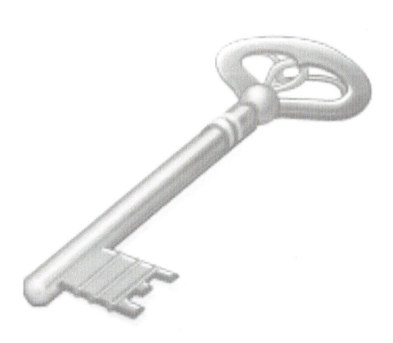

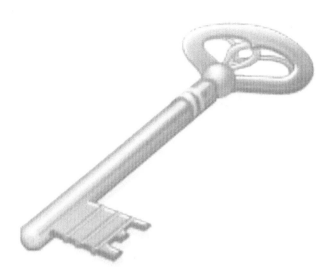

78

The Identity Key: This is my favorite! Can you color it special, unique, and make it one of a kind? Can you see it in your imagination? When the KING gives you a key, no one can take it away!

What are the new things that you are going to do and create? Can you draw them on this page and unlock new ideas with this key? Go into your imagination and ask the KING. HE will help! Draw what you see, hear, taste, touch and smell.

Made in United States
North Haven, CT
24 March 2025

67203542R00051